All About Children

Elaine M. Ward

DEDICATION

To Ann McCutchan, who weaves her words and music into sounds and sights of beauty and wonder, gifts for the "starchild" in each of us.

ALL ABOUT CHILDREN
By Elaine Ward
Copyright © 1999 Educational Ministries, Inc.
ISBN 1-57438-037-0

Educational Ministries, Inc.
165 Plaza Dr.
Prescott, AZ 86303
800-221-0910

Table of Contents

INTRODUCTION

This book is All About Children who are "all-about," here and there, everywhere touching, tasting, smelling, seeing, hearing, laughing, crying, running, jumping, curious, eager to learn—to "fly."'

There are two gifts we can give children: roots and wings. The glad contentment and thanksgiving of a child comes from the roots they have established. Children first put down their roots at home as they learn trust from their relationship with their parents and caretakers. The "climate" adults provide helps children grow socially, emotionally, intellectually, and spiritually. The "rain" and "sunshine" of a smile, a gesture, the tone of voice, the touch, nourish the faith, love, and security necessary for spiritual development.

> *Children are born with "wings:"*
> *"I want to fly! I want to fly!"*
> *This is my daughter Susan's cry.*
> *I pick her up not asking, "Why?"*
> *Flinging her feet into the sky.*
> *If Susan wants, let Susan try.*
> *Too soon she'll be too "wise" to fly!*

The author of Hebrews wrote that some have entertained angels unaware. Children can be "angels, opening doors to encounter God. Several years ago Stan Stewart and Dennis Benson wrote a wonderful book called <u>The Ministry of the Child</u> in which they named their angels "Starchildren."

Each of us has a "starchild" within, blessed by God. Aware of these angels among us, they minister to us, for the quality of childlikeness is eternal, ever fresh, seeing with wonder. Their ministry invites us to play, to see the creative handiwork of God, and to delight in the Lord.

Jesus said, "Let the children come to me," and "Unless you become as a little child you will not be aware of, and thus not enter to the kingdom of God" (paraphrase).

So as you read, share, and discuss the content of <u>All About Children</u>, may you experience of joy of becoming as a little child, loved and delighted by God, and from this gladness, live abundantly with children all about.

Teachers, parents, pastors, and other persons who care about children benefit from coming "all together in one place" (Acts 2:1). Written in the format of sessions, possible suggestions for gathering are a weekend retreat, an evening study group or for training on Sunday morning. If this is not possible, use the sessions as for teacher training or as a basis for a sermon and/or service of worship "all about children."

The format of the sessions contains the theme, Scripture texts, content to be read, reflected, and discussed, and activities to do.

Oh, the wonder of a child...
Sometimes meek,
Sometimes mild,
Sometimes wiggling,
Sometimes wild.
Oh, the wonder of a child...

Always exciting,
Wanting to know,
Learning and loving,
And eager to grow.
Oh, the wonder of a child...

Too wondrous for labeling,
Each different in size,
In skills, understanding,
And all a surprise!
Oh, the wonder of a child...

Amazed and bewildered,
Perplexed and beguiled,
Adults join in wonder
And love of ... a child!

Belong

Children Need To Belong

To belong means we were loved by God before the beginning. We learn that sense of belonging in the church through the sacrament of baptism in which God says, "You are my child." Belonging to God is belonging to a community of faith and to the world, for "the earth is the Lord's and everything in it."

A deep sense of belonging to a beloved community of faith is an important part of children's faith development, for children have a need to belong, to feel accepted, and to participate as a member of their faith community.

God made a covenant with Abraham: "I will be your God and you will be my people." In the church school children experience this covenant, this sense of belonging.

All of us are born with a longing for a relationship with God, with one another, and with all creation. The child's greatest fear is separation from the care-giver. In the book The Runaway Bunny, the bunny expresses his desire to run away, which children experience when their wishes are thwarted or they feel unloved. The mother rabbit, recognizing the bunny's need to express his frustration, responds with imagination and love, showing and telling him how she will find him until the bunny, knowing that he truly belongs, replies, "Then I might as well stay here and be your bunny."'

Another book children love is <u>Where the Wild Things Are</u>, identifying with Max who becomes a wild thing and commands those "wild things," such as the emotion of anger, until he wants to return "to where someone loves him best of all."'

When Jesus said, "Let the children come unto me," he knew about the need for the little, lost, and lonely to belong. When he spoke of love, he told the story of the Loving Father and the prodigal son. The Father waited for his son to return, as God waits for our return. It is too good to be true, but it is the love for which we all yearn.

Lucas, age five, driving to church one Sunday morning with his mother, got out of the car, saw and smelled the roses growing in the yard around the church, looked up at the church steeple rising high into the sky, and said to his mother, "This is a good place to be!" Trey on the other hand had been away from church for a long time and when he entered with his father, looked up at him and frowned. Anxiously he asked, "Do you think God has forgotten who I am?"

The child's need to belong is satisfied in the church school among his/her peers and in the sanctuary where they are welcomed in worship. The church educator's role is to assist children in explaining what will happen. Depending upon the age of the children and their attention span, children may attend part of the service or the complete service some of the time.

In church school children learn the hymns, discuss the Scripture text as it applies to their concerns, memorize the Doxology and Gloria Patri, be taught how to read the psalms and other responses, and participate in "passing the peace" (extending hands to one another while saying the words, "The peace of God be with you").

Children sense their "belonging" when they are welcomed entering the church, at coffee hour or meals at church, church fairs or bazaars in which they are invited to work, setting the tables, putting out chairs, serving in a booth or other activities that involve them.

When the minister is comfortable with children, they experience a deeper sense of belonging through this special relationship at "children's time at the altar" or other times. Some churches conduct a special Children's Day worship service in which children serve as ushers, choir, and/or liturgist. I know of one church where one of the sixth graders of the confirmation class preached the day they were confirmed. Retreats held for older children allow more time to establish the sense of belonging.

Because belonging is so important, it is well to be aware that children need "things" that belong to them: dolls, stuffed animals, pets, "my" bicycle, "my" bed, etc. When we allow belonging, stewardship out of love follows more naturally than when we force "sharing." In class, however, only one's turn belongs to them. We say, "Carrie is using the ... now. You may have a turn later" and follow through.

To understand children's need to belong and their other needs we wish to know the characteristics of childhood:

Children are:

1. Active

2. Literal, concrete:

Sarah, age five, said, looking out at the rain, "Rain is God's ... what are those runny things from your eyes?" Her mother replied, "Tears?" "Yes, tears," Sarah agreed. There was silence and then Sarah said, "April must be a very sad month." Again there was silence. In a few minutes Charles, age seven, said, "Well, I'm not sure they are God's tears." Then a long pause before he said, "I know the truth. I really do." Another pause and "I think I know the truth," and after another long pause, "No one knows the truth."

3. Imaginative

4. Curious

5. Imitators

6. Dependent: children want to be safe.

Anticipating Christmas the children were recalling memories of past Christmases when Robert said, "I like thinking about the things that are done. Sometimes bad things can happen. You can die or your parents divorce, scarey things like that, so I just like things that have happened. They are safe."

7. Independent

8. Playful

9. Inattentive

10. Expressive: children have a gift with words.

Steven, age four, was cleaning up. "I like the way you are cleaning up, Steven," the adult said. Steven replied, "We always clean up ... Sometimes."

11. Eager to learn and try:

The child was to write five spelling words five times. She had finished three of the words when her teacher said, "Susan, you have two to go." Susan looked up at her teacher and said, "Teacher, why do you notice what I haven't done, rather than what I do?"

12. Creative

13. Unique, different

14. Full of wonder

15. Self-centered/loving:

"You can't go away. I will miss you too much. I love you," she told me and when I had been gone three months, she said on the telephone, "Come home, Elaine! You made a mistake." "How can I come home? I have a job." "Quit your job. You made a mistake. I love you."

16. Sensitive:

He wore an apron and played with the doll and the other boys laughed. With time they would learn the importance of nurturing and shared responsibility.

17. Live in the present:

Bradley, age five, brought his picture to his mother. He was so proud of his drawing that he had written his name on it. Ignoring the picture, she exclaimed over his name, "You wrote your own name! Just like a big first grader, you wrote your own name!" Bradley crumpled his picture in his hand and silently walked away, wondering what was wrong with being a five-year-old now.

18. Honest:

In her enthusiasm the teacher exclaimed, "Isn't it fun to listen? Isn't it fun to share? Isn't it fun to take turns?" to which the child replied, "Teacher, I hate fun!"

19. Uninhibited:

Lauren expressed it: "In school it's what you are that counts."

20. Learn through their senses: Children "see" because they keep their hearts and minds open. They appreciate and use and learn through their senses. Annie Dillard in <u>Pilgrim at Tinker Creek</u> writes of having wished all of her adult life to see the cemented case of a caddisfly larva.

One day she was sitting with the young daughter of friends. "What's this?" she asked, picking up such a case on the pebbled bottom of the stream. "I wanted to say as I recognized the prize she held, 'That is a memento mori for people who read too much.'"

Learning Opportunities:

1. Enjoy the finger play "If I Were the Church:"

   If I were the church
   My church bells would ring (swing arms as bells)
   "Come everyone," I'd gladly sing.
   If I were the church,
   I'd stretch my doors wide (open arms)
   And welcome everyone inside (close arms).
   If I were the church,
   But I am you see,
   For the church is people,
   You, and you, and me. (point to self, others, and self again)[4]

2. Prepare centers for young children to "play church" by using dress-up clothes to get ready to come to church, build churches with blocks, make a mural with pictures of people at church, play with church people puppets, put together puzzles of church pictures, sing songs about church, hear stories of church people, and "attend church" with Bibles.

3. Brainstorm the ways children learn based on their characteristics.

4. Read the following story and discuss how you can help children experience a sense of belonging at church:

The guest preacher shared with the congregation his work with youth who used and sold heroin. Accompanying his talk the congregation viewed it on screen and the pain and confusion were overwhelming. During the coffee hour that followed a young woman came up to him, carrying a very young baby in her arms. "I was very moved by your story of Tom." Suddenly she looked down at her baby and began to cry, "How can I raise him to have a good life? How can I be sure he doesn't get carried away like your young friend?" Everyone stopped talking. It was a closely knit church and when one part of its body suffered, everyone felt it. The young woman continued, "I had him baptized last week. How can I live up to those vows?" At that point one older man walked over and took the baby in his arms, gently rocking him and saying, "Jenny, we—the members of the church took some vows last week also. It will be hard for you, but you will do your best. It may even be harder for us to remember how this baby is part of our family and needs our care, but we are going to try. We love you both and with God's help we can all make it."[5]

5. Have books available to take home and read. The following books are recommended:

David Heller, Talking to Your Child About God (New York: Bantam, 1988).

Patricia W. Van Ness, Transforming Bible Study with Children (Nashville, TN: Abingdon, 1991).

Polly Berrien Berends, Gently Lead (New York: Harper, 1991).

Elaine M. Ward, Children and Drama; Children and Bible Stories; Children and Prayer; Answering Children's Faith Questions; Old Testament Stories; New Testament Stories; Growing with the Bible (Prescott, AZ: Educational Ministries).

Elaine M. Ward, Love in a Lunchbox: Poems and Parables for Children's Worship, (Nashville, TN: Abingdon, 1996).

Rick Osborne, Talking to Your Children about God (New York: HarperCollins).

---

[1] Margaret Wise Brown, The Runaway Bunny (New York: Harper Collins, 1977).

[2] Maurice Sendak, Where the Wild Things Are (New York: Harper Collins, 1988).

[3] See Ward, Children and Worship (Prescott, AZ: Educational Ministries, 1993) for 62 ways to involve children in worship.

[4] Elaine M. Ward, Be and Say a Fingerplay (Prescott, AZ: Educational Ministries, 1981).

[5] Dennis C. Benson and Stan J. Stewart, The Ministry of the Child (Nashville, TN: Abingdon, 1979), pp. 116-117.

TRUST

Children

Need

Trust

I want the right to make mistakes,
I want the right to learn and try,
To grow a trust inside myself,
To talk, and laugh, and cry.
I want the right to parents' care,
And people who will understand,
And whether I am right or wrong
Will love me as God planned.

The first task of childhood is to learn to trust. When children have a sense of belonging, they trust. Jesus called God "Abba" which means Daddy, the sign of trust, the talk of a child who is at home with God, the cry of faith. In these words Jesus removed prayer from the formal institutionalized formula to that of intimate trust in the midst of life, a personal, loving relationship with God.

An intuitive seven-year-old girl was taken from her mother who had subjected her to the hazards of her own uncertainties and unhealthy way of life as a prostitute. After a few months in her new home she was asked, "What do you like best at school?" "Oh," she cried, "as it was in the beginning, is now, and ever shall be, world without end. Amen. I never knew that there was anything that was in the beginning and always would be ... it makes one feel so nice and safe."

Identity has its roots in dependability, love, and nurture, the making and keeping of contracts. As children recognize the faithfulness of those who keep their promises, they begin to make and keep promises, for children trust actions, deeds, more than words. Whether children affirm, accept, and appreciate life, or deny, suspect, or fear it, depends on how they are affirmed, accepted, and appreciated, or ignored, criticized, and deceived.

Children depend upon parents and teachers to "be there." A woman who lived near her minister and his wife sometimes babysat with their children overnight. One night the two-year-old son awoke, crying for his daddy. There was no comforting the boy until the woman remembered the pastor's cassette of sermons recorded for the ill. Together they listened to it. The small boy, recognizing his father's voice, was comforted and went back to sleep.

To trust God's providence and promise as a child means to receive God's love and presence, and when children trust and feel secure they can teach us trust.

The greatest gift we can give a child is to model trust. Trust in God, faith, comes to and through the child as we share with one another our love of God and God's love to us.

When the child came to his teacher, crying, she put him on her lap and asked, "Did you have an accident?" She comforted the child and the child trusted his teacher. He felt safe and loved in her lap. Then he stopped crying and replied, "Christopher hit me, but I'd like to think that it was an accident, because he's my best friend."

Teaching a class in seminary on "Ministry with Children," an older student wrote a paper in class, concerning the death of his daughter, his firstborn child. Dying at the age of fifteen months, it was a shattering experience with long range reverberations. He was unaware that she was a diabetic. No one had told him this at her birth and yet he felt he should have known, for looking back, things were not quite right. After she went into a coma, he thought his prayer was not earnest enough and offered himself in her stead. When she died, he turned on God in his bitterness. "One day," he wrote, "I became aware of an eight-year-old girl that attended Chapel services, always sitting at the very front and eyeing my activities as organist and choir director with intensity. Eventually we became friends. When I learned that she was dying from a form of cancer, I began to feel my bitterness anew. But this eight-year-old shared with me her trust in spite of her impending death, her absolute trust in the justness and righteousness of God, and her desire that I play for her funeral service. Her faith caused me to renew my relationship with God, based on trust rather than selfishness, that has continued to grow to this present day, even leading me to commitment and dedication to serve a true and living God."

Think of the trustworthiness of God, creating a world of order: Earth is part of the cosmos of one hundred billion galaxies rushing through space without collision, day always following night, seasons in sequence, the working of our physical bodies!

My son used to give swimming lessons to young children. The first thing he taught them was to trust the water. As he held the child on its back with his hands supporting their body, they relaxed until they trusted him enough to let him remove his hands and they floated, trusting the water and their bodies to hold them.

Clark was only four, but he could create Goliath headaches, confusion, and chaos. Through the year the teacher had tried to give him love and limits, but it was hard to see any change, for the habits were deep. One morning the children were talking with their teacher about what they wanted to be. "When I grow up, I want to be a lawyer," said Alan. "I want to be a nurse," said Susan. "I'm going to be a daddy," declared Dan. "I want to be ... I want to be..." Clark began. "What do you want to be, Clark?" his teacher asked, encouraging him to speak. "I want to be..." There was a long pause. "I want to be ... a good boy. I want God to make me a good boy so my daddy will like me."

Children's self-image is based on their ability to trust and to be seen as worthy of trust. The sense of feeling inadequate limits learning and the love of life.

Trust is a tender thing, a risk,
The greatest risk that life can bring,
The pain, the fear that love will die,
And yet I know not trust, nor love,
Unless I try.

Trust is built on love, but we do not learn love or love in the abstract. Children need experiences of love before they can understand the words, "God loves you." They need models of trust. When parents brought their children to Jesus, he took them up in her arms and blessed them (Mark 10:16). He performed the act of love more often than he talked about it.

"How long have you been teaching?" the boy asked. The teacher sat down, trying to recall how many years it had been. They had flown past so swiftly. It was twenty years since she had first walked into that class and loved each child. The child who asked the question waited while she was remembering. Then the teacher smiled and put her arm around his waist, as she said, "I have been teaching for twenty years." His eyes grew large as he exclaimed, "You must do it by heart!" That was exactly how she did it.

One teacher recalled how her grandmother walked and talked with God. She was a constant example of hope and trust in God because she believed in God's goodness and love. Whenever the teacher encountered adversity, she remembered the way her grandmother lived.

Our presence as church educators in the classroom models God's love, for as one child told his mother, "God couldn't come today so God sent our teacher."

A nurse told of the first time she sat at the bedside of a dying child. She sat from duty. Before she died, this seven-year-old, who had suffered for five years with leukemia, found the final energy to sit up and say: "The angels—they're so beautiful! Mommy, can you see them? Do you hear them singing? I've never heard such beautiful singing!" The nurse in her despair cried out later to God, "Don't you care, God?" and heard the words, "Yes, I care and it is because I care that you are there. And I am there too."

The greatest gift we can give a child is to model trust, to be there to cry with the child, hold and comfort the child, and when frustrated remind the child, "I am here. I will help you ... if you need me."

Learning Opportunities:

1. Read the following story and discuss children's need for trust:

I once had a friend named "Bear." He was a big, black, furry puppy who greeted me each morning when I took my daily walk around the neighborhood. No matter how grouchy or frightened or sad I, or any other walker, was that morning, the persistence of the puppy who did not know any better than to be happy and to run joyously to greet every stranger, finally won us over. Bear was the friend of all the neighborhood. Shaking with excitement, he enjoyed every scratch, hug, or gushy word of love. He reminded me of my next-door neighbor, Sarah. Sarah was three and she knew no stranger. As a small child she would plop herself in your lap, unmindful of wrinkling dresses or freshly pressed pants or unextended invitations, feeling completely wanted and welcomed. Wiggling with joy, she too enjoyed every touch and hug and gushy word of love.

Life, unfortunately, teaches us to beware of "Bears," for some dogs bark and bite, and someday Sarah will be demure and polite and blush when invited to sit on someone's lap, using her head instead of her heart. Yet to enter the Kingdom of God as a little child is permission to be as spontaneous and trusting as Bear and Sarah, without the worry about what people will think, as friendly as a big, boisterous, shaggy dog or a small, satisfied, smiling Sarah.

2. Recall your favorite teacher and ask, "Why do I remember that person? What kind of model was she or he? What was his/her most outstanding quality?

3. Look at pictures of Jesus and name what you see. Name two of the strengths the picture depicts.

4. Divide into groups of three, each with a reporter. Read Mark 1:16-20 and write a want-ad for the newspaper, seeking a church educator for children. List the requirements and responsibilities, the opportunities and benefits of this employment. Be imaginative.

5. Close your eyes and sit in silence, recalling your most memorable learning experiences as teacher or learner, inside or outside the classroom, positive or negative. Jot down experiences as they come to mind and choose one to share with the group.

6. Read: Give a group of people a certain destination to be reached in a certain number of hours. Those who travel separately will be late and tired. If they walk with another, they will be less late and less tired, and if they do it competitively or with singing in unison and rhythm, they will hardly be tired at all. Enjoying together doubles and triples one's single efforts. Discuss the advantages of teaching in a team.

God

Children

Need

To Know

God

Jesus said, "Let the children come to me."

I may not hear God's voice
Or see or touch God's face,
But through the love you show to me,
I know God's in this place.

I may not know the names for God,
But I can feel God's care
Through loving people who show me
That God is everywhere.

Trust is based on knowing God's love through people who love us and through our faith imagination. Faith imagination is a bridge to God and the more developed, the deeper the awareness of God can grow. Jesus told parables, metaphors encouraging faith imagination, to show us God's presence. Through telling stories he showed his trust in images, gifts from God, and children think in images.

To know God is the work of a lifetime, for a relationship with God is life's most essential work. God is love because love is concrete and relational, but love is not God because that is abstract.

Knowing God is different from knowing *about* God.

Preschool. Knowing about God includes hearing stories about Jesus at Christmas as a baby, growing as children do, and stories of his love for people. Teaching simple songs of praise, reading verses from the Bible appropriate to their age, and having conversations about God are important to the preschool child.

In preschool years children participate in family customs: rituals for Sundays and holidays, birthdays, prayer times at meal and bedtime, and spontaneously throughout the day. Many children participate in the church's customs, as well, witnessing baptism, hearing organ music, seeing the actions of the worshipers, watching the Advent wreath be lighted, figures placed in the creche, and "passing the peace."

Elementary children continue to grow, wanting to know more and more and giving up earlier misconceptions, for experiencing religious emotions (heart) before understanding religious thoughts, (head), children are more like adults in feelings than in concepts. For children the sense of wonder, of imagination, is more important than facts, information, and memorized words. Through play, music, stories, games, reading, writing, drama, dance, and discussion, faith imagination and curiosity are fed.

As children develop they encounter both success and failure which affects their sense of self-worth. A child's faith can become a source of strength in times of fear, stress, and disappointment. Erik Erikson studied children and their emotional development and labeled their tasks as trust, faith, and identity.

Pre-adolescents, around the age of eleven, can think abstractly, have a sense of history, and begin to understand the meaning of commitment. The task of teaching children about God is the responsibility of the parents and the faith community. The goals for such teaching vary within church communities, be they to learn the content of the Bible, commitment to Christ, or loyalty to and participation in the life of the church, its worship, education, and service of love in the world.

These goals vary but I believe that whatever the goal, it is based on knowing God. It is the gift and grace of God. Knowing God, our relationship with God, is a personal experience. Thus it is unpredictable.

Prayer is our relationship with God, the unseen, silent Source of our life and energy, who loves us with unconditional love. Therefore helping children pray is crucial to their faith development. Children understand the vocabulary of the faith at the level of their age, some understanding the words, others intuiting the meaning, and some being confused, for this is in the area of knowing "about" God, while "knowing God" in prayer is the sense of being loved by a Love beyond belief, providing a sense of confidence and unity with all creation.

Edward Robinson conducted a study of the religious experiences of childhood and discovered children as young as three and four experiencing this sense of identity, wonder, peace, and gratitude. For some of the children it happened in creation, being with flowers, trees, water, sky, animals. For others it occurred in the beauty of the sanctuary, listening to its music, looking through the stained glass windows and the lighted candles in a darkened place, and in the security of belonging to a people.

Hearts full of love, children's expressions of praise and thanksgiving in their own words come closer to knowing God than memorized prayers, knowing about God. "For what would you like to thank God?" invites children to think and express their own particular things that comes from their personal relationship with God.

When we do say prayers aloud for children, we address God as one who is loving, understands our feelings of fear and hurt and anger, and is always near to love us. As children grow they will learn that prayer is listening, as well. In the class we are aware of individual differences. Some children can sit quietly and wait. Others are in constant motion. Knowing this, my first year of teaching kindergarten in a Christian weekday school, I prayed aloud briefly. After a few weeks, when Debbie learned to trust me, she said in a frustrated voice, "Why do you say 'Amen' just as I am beginning to pray?"

The years of childhood are the years for feeding wonder and imagination, which feed religious experience through prayer and poetry, books, stories, song, music, nature, and worship, important to children's spiritual development.

Children see and think with their imagination. The burning bush that was not consumed in the story of Moses is not a miracle to children, but the fact of fire is. However, children know the difference between real and make believe, even when they prefer the latter. "When I go to bed, I get stronger," Charles said, as he jumped into and out of his bed again and again. He had been told that sleep was essential for growing but he made sense of it with his own three year old mind. Children are "literalists of imagination." With time they will sort out reality and fantasy, not by ignoring fantasy which is an important part of their development, but as they experience which is which. The child will continue to make mud pies even though he will not try to eat them.

Children learn from people and what children see and experience them modeling. They learn to pray alone and in community, in the worship in church school and sanctuary and at home.

In the early years children are the center of their world. All things are related to them. They are the cause of what happens, be it an argument between parents, a divorce, a death, or a celebration of a birthday.

POINT-OF-VIEW

The world is full of many things,
Of sky and land and sea,
Of sun and moon,
Of bird and bee,
And in the
Center
Me

Childhood is a period of "affinitive faith," of belonging and participating in relationship with others. The child learns through experience, then images and stories, and finally abstract concepts around the age of fourteen. Childhood is the time when the religion of the heart dominates.

A five-year-old begged her parents to allow her to stay up until midnight on Shavuot, the celebration of the giving of the Torah. She begged and pleaded until at last her mother agreed to a compromise. "You are only five and you cannot stay up until midnight. When you are ten we will let you do it." Tearfully the girl replied, "But when I am ten, I won't believe it any more." We call it preclinical naivete—that time in childhood when we believe to be true whatever the significant authority figures in our lives tell us is true.

Before she was six, Linda one day noticed a butterfly in flight and felt drawn to it. She followed it and suddenly everything seemed to open up around her. She felt filled with clarity of vision, joy and warmth throughout her whole body. Bursting into tears, she ran to her mother, shouting, "Mommy, I know God!" Later she told her mother, "It was not an explanation, it was an exclamation."[1]

It is time to bring religious experience, all of life, life in the spirit, back into the church, where it originated. These are the "roots" we can give our children, deep roots of abiding love from God through Christ.

Unburdened by logic or disillusionment, children are free to see freshly, to be creative. Children are co-creators with God from birth but the vision fades as they grow. It is then the sacred story told and enfleshed can offer them true hope for their faith imagination. So children grow ... in faith, hope, and love. "And the greatest of these is love."

Learning Opportunities:

1. Make a list of your goals for the religious development of children and discuss the religious questions they ask.

2. Play "word association." Name the following words and ask participants to write whatever words, thoughts, memories, feelings come to mind: faith, minister, teacher, God, Bible, Jesus, story, church, love, hope, children, church school, adventure, and any others you wish to add.

3. Reflect and discuss who or what was influential in your religious nurture and development as a child and what or who is influential now.

4. Invite God into your faith imagination by sitting still and letting go your own needs and expectations to listen to God. Savor God's unconditional love as you sit in silence. Soak in God's love as a fresh rain refreshes the thirsty ground. Pray "Thy will be done."

5. List the blessings in your life and write a prayer of praise and thanksgiving, using your faith imagination.

6. Sing "Spirit of the Living Lord."

[1]Sofia Cavalletti, The Religious Potential of the Child (New York: Paulist Press, 1979), pp. 35-36.

Limits

Children

Need

Limits

"You shall teach (these commandments) diligently to your children" (Deuteronomy 6:7).

Children who live with brothers and sisters know there are limits. "If I get two pieces of cake, he may not get one." Children who attend school, church, or any social gathering know there are limits. "We take turns." "God loves you and God loves Susie. I can't let you hit Susie."

John Donne's "No man is an island" is learned young. The younger the better, for all of us are limited. Children need to learn limits and become aware of the rights of others.

There are limits to the number of paints or crayons or paper, limits to space, and every artist knows there are freely chosen limits within which to work. Teachers too have limitations of talent, skills, understandings. There is no shortage on limitations.

Yet boundaries give children a sense of security. Limits are necessary for reasons of safety, health, care of others, and concern for property. Young children are taught "rules." As they grow older they learn "principles." Rules set boundaries (The Ten Commandments). Principles apply to how we treat other people. "You shall love your neighbor as yourself" (Leviticus 19:17). Principles are based on wisdom and love, but even rules require personal interpretation at times. Until the child is old enough, children need our help in living with rules creatively. Learning limits is seen as discipline, related to the word "disciple."

Before adolescence children make decisions or act spontaneously based on consequences (reward or punishment, satisfaction of their own needs, and winning approval by others). All along they learn through the models they see, the love (and law) they experience, and the literature that helps them transcend themselves. Storytelling, role-playing, films, simulation games, prayer, help children choose their values. But children need practice in making decisions, respecting the consequences of their actions, and living with limits. They learn the skills of self-control, cooperation, and compromise on a limited scale. With time, teaching, and learning the positive use of words, external control becomes internal.

As church educators we ask, "How do we help children live with limits?"

- **Children learn sensitivity through self-esteem rather than force**. Punishment causes children to want revenge, to get even, rather than to do right. When authority is loving and helpful, accepting and affirming the other, helping the child to self-discipline, it is heard, appreciated, and learned. Explanations begin early and praise is a powerful tool. So are positive reinforcement and a sense of humor.

    A mother tried positive reinforcement, negative reinforcement, and then discussion. Finally in desperation she put the child in the closet, immediately feeling guilty and calling, "What are you doing?" "I'm spitting on your shoes!" the child replied. The mother waited a moment and then asked, "Now what are you doing?" "I'm spitting on your dress." Exasperated, she tried one more time. "Now what are you doing?" Her child, undisturbed, replied, "Waiting for more spit."

- Sometimes the consequences of unacceptable behavior may involve **depriving children of something important.** Coloring on the wall may eliminate crayons for awhile.

- **Children need routine:**

    The forecast was for rain. The sky was growing darker by the minute. I suggested to the children that we go outside to play now, adjusting our schedule, for our routine was to go outside after we had eaten our snack. After using our allotted time on the playground we returned to our room. The children were puzzled and concerned. "What is the matter, Alicia?" I asked. She replied, "I'm hungry. Have we eaten already?"

    Routine is doing things in predictable order. Children need order they can count on. "I don't know what time it is," the three-year-old said, getting up from her nap at the childcare center, "but I know Daddy will be here soon because he always comes to take me home after my nap."

In an instant culture—instant food, instant pleasure, instant likes and dislikes—we expect to reap immediate rewards. It is difficult to wait, but some things cannot be hurried.

- **Look for solutions rather than explanations.**
  Sarah accidently fell while running with her brother, Charles. When no one came to her rescue immediately, she was about to get up and go on about playing until her aunt entered the scene, asking authoritatively, "What is going on?" Sarah, feeling accused, became defensive and cried, "Charles made me do it." The question, "What happened?" called for an explanation and a judge, yet no judge sleeps in the same house with his prisoner. Rather than looking for explanations, look for solutions.

- **Change behavior with distraction.**
  When Emma's father called her there was no movement on the part of Emma. "Emma, we have to go now." Emma did not hear or at least pretended not to hear. "Emma, one, two, three..." Wearily, the parent counted with frustration and then, suddenly, smiled, picking up his daughter in his arms, hugging her with love, and carrying her out of the room while singing. The distraction worked. One day, with time and love, Emma will move on her own.

- **Repeat instructions.** Come to the child. Look into his/her eyes and speak slowly and distinctly. Before interfering, give the child time to act on his/her own. Clear, calm, consistent directions, given with reasonable, loving authority help eliminate the small frustrations that grow into large ones. Give directions in brief and positive terms: "Walk in the halls." "Use inside voices." "You may have a turn when Clair is finished." "The blocks are kept on the floor." "The milk spilled, it needs wiping up." "Hitting is not acceptable here."

- **When correcting, talk in private** to avoid humiliating the child. When discipline is firm, loving, clear, creative, children take a leap toward their own self-discipline which is the basis for joyous and abundant growth. Haim Ginott once said, "A dash of dignified discipline may prevent a pound of punishment."

- **Use firm limit-setting** by recognizing the feeling ("I know you would like to..."), set the limit ("but you may not because..."), and provide an alternative ("but we could..." or "what if you...?").

- **Arrange the room and choose activities with the needs of children in mind**, providing a quiet corner for "Time Out" when children need it.

- **Plan activities that provide an outlet for children's pent-up feelings**. Have change-of-pace activities. Children become tired from sitting.

- **Help children substitute words for destructive behavior,** as well as using water, clay dough, finger painting, walking, and other physical action.

- **Expectations of the child's performance change** when the child is sick, or learning to cope with the absence of a parent or the addition of a sibling, returning from a hospital stay, or dealing with death, the lack of sleep or food, stress or anxiety within the family.

- **Remain calm.** Children's wants are greater than their need to please. Children live in the here and now, therefore delayed gratification is not easy. When they are angry, reason is ignored. With time, patience, and modeling, children learn more appropriate ways to express their emotions.

- **Listen.** Help children learn that there are other ways than screaming or inappropriate behavior to get attention. Talk about what you saw happen and listen to the child's response. Church educators model and articulate that winning is not as important as learning how to communicate and live with others in love.

- **The rules of teaching are but three: love, limit, and let them be.**
  The father came to the rabbi, distraught because his son had turned away from religion. "What shall I do?" he asked the rabbi. "Do you love your son?" asked the rabbi. The father replied, "Of course I love my son." "Then love him more."
  Discipline comes from the word "disciple," who follows and imitates the one he loves and respects.

- **When communicating speak slowly,** using only the words that are essential to your meaning, and speak clearly, enunciating your words carefully and not talking down to children. Get their attention before you speak.

- **Use imagination.** Imagine yourself in the child's place. Express the child's feelings. "I know you would like to stay. You are having fun but it is time for the whole class to gather to sing together."

- **Help children learn to use words in place of fists.** "I think you are really angry right now." "I am not for biting." "The rule is..." It takes children time to learn how to manage their feelings which motivate action. In a relationship of trust we can assure children that they can count on us. "You can hold my hand. I will help you not to hurt yourself or another."

- **Invite children to "act out" various feelings, using words.** "How do you feel when someone hits (grabs, makes fun of, kicks, etc.) you?"

- **Sing thoughts and feelings**.

- **Choose a few necessary rules** and make sure children understand what you mean and mean what you say. Be firm without harshness. Be consistent without inflexibility. When infractions occur talk about the consequences in terms children can understand.

- With young children **teach them how to offer to trade** a toy for something they want. Use a timer or other system for taking turns. Use puppets, stories, and drama to practice actions in the classroom.

- **Older children can learn to send "I" messages about what they are feeling.** Repeat what is heard. Take responsibility for your own part and brainstorm solutions.

- **Discuss** which of the following "solutions" they use when in conflict: pray, tell an adult, tell a friend, talk to the one with whom you are in conflict, ignore it, and any that the children suggest.

- **Sit beside students who are easily distracted** and away from people/things that distract them. Pair a parent or youth helper with a child who needs extra attention.

Learning Opportunities:

1. Reflect, discuss or write, and share: Discipline is... What is the opposite of discipline? How was I disciplined as a child? What would I change? Do I discipline to maintain order or to help children solve problems? What are children learning from my mode of discipline? What is my response when I have not seen the behavior another child is reporting or when I hear a child cry and I have not seen what happened? Who are my models for disciplining?

2. Invite a child psychologist, preschool teacher or director, and parent to present a panel discussion on "limits." Invite each participant to write a question concerning discipline for the panelist to read aloud and respond to.

3. Spend time in praying for your children, yourself in the classroom, and specific children who need positive discipline.

4. Discuss particular problems church educators present. Role-play teacher and child and ask other participants to observe in order to talk about what might be changed.

Faith

Children

Need

Models

Of Faith

"Be doers of the world and not merely hearers..." (James 1:22)

Made in the image of God, who is the source of creative love and compassion, and having been given the gift of the Holy Spirit, we seek to discern the movements of the Holy Spirit in our life and pray for the energy and obedience to share that movement with children.

In our love we model God's love and in that modeling (caring, listening, sharing) we show that God is love. Because the religious experience is fundamentally an expression of love and the child's infinite need for love cannot be satisfied by human love, no child is loved to the degree he/she wants and needs, thus, in contact with God, who is Love, the child finds the nourishment he/she needs to grow.

One of our discoveries is the beauty and power of prayer. The church educator's relationship with God is the most powerful tool in the classroom for church ministry is not a science, a methodology, but an art, the celebration and proclamation of the joy of Resurrection in action. As guides gently leading children to their true hope and joy through their deepest longings, we "dance with God."

It is not presentation of doctrine or biblical knowledge, rites or beliefs that conveys "religious education" but Spirit-filled behavior. When we put spirit higher than intellect (for it includes both intellect and feelings), we assist children's authentic human growth. We call it faith ... possibility in God.

As church educators our task is helping children hear, see, question, and pray to arrive at their own personal faith, an awareness of the presence of God, an adventure of the spirit.

We begin by seeking, which leads to the power of prayer, through which we find God and return to "teach," prepare the place of possibility. All religious teaching begins with God. The Bible, Jesus, sacraments, worship, prayer are all based on who God is for us. The purpose of religious education is a relationship with God, to know the presence of God here and now.

Children learn through relationships. Research findings suggest that there is a positive relationship between the self-concept of the teacher and the cognitive growth of the children in her charge. The way the learner acquires religious content exerts a more powerful influence than the content itself.

Because there is no "one right way" of teaching, church educators may take comfort in the quality of being flexible. Most of us prefer to learn in creative ways rather than by authority, although we do not exclude having authorities for anchoring, and using other methods of learning, as well.

One of the effective characteristics of a model is listening.
Todd was listening to two older boys. When his mother came, he said, "They were cheating." "No, Todd," she replied, "you must have misunderstood. Cheating is bad." "Don't say that to me. They were cheating." "No, Todd, they were not cheating. Cheating is bad," she replied. Todd became more upset. "They were so cheating!" "I do not want you to talk back to me."

The mother had not heard or seen what had happened. I had. The truth was that the teenage boys had been cheating, cheating good naturally, but Todd was right. The trouble was that Todd's mother did not trust Todd to have his facts straight. Nor did she bother to find out if Todd was correct. She was so concerned to teach Todd that cheating was bad, she did not listen to the feelings behind his words.

A missionary child came to Boston on furlough with her family. Her whole life had been spent in places distant from Boston and she eagerly looked forward to being in a real school and in a geography class that would help her learn about other places. Her enthusiasm and joy was great when she was able to answer all the questions on the oral geography test. The teacher had said, "Answer only what you know, what you, yourself, have seen. What city do you know? What river do you know? What mountain do you know?" Each Boston child replied, "Boston, Boston, Boston," and when the child said "Bagdad," the teacher gave her a stern look and a stern reminder to speak the truth. To the second question the children answered, "The Charles River, Charles River, Charles River," and she said, "The Euphrates." The teacher became more visibly upset. When each Boston children replied, "Blue Hill Mountain, Blue Hill, Blue Hill," she said, "Ararat." The teacher, now infuriated, said, "Two falsehoods, and now a third. Such places you have never seen."

To listen involves the heart as well as the ears. What an exciting class that might have been and what a rewarding experience for the child and for the entire class if the teacher had listened with her imagination.

She was only three, going on four, so when she asked the question, "Was Jesus in your class when he was a little boy?" his teacher was not offended. Nor did she laugh. She only shook her head "no," appreciating what she said and hugging her, as the child lovingly replied, "Poor Jesus. Never to have you as his teacher!"

The first grader looked up at her teacher one Sunday morning, smiling, as she said, "You are just like Jesus." Her teacher swallowed hard and returned her smile. She asked, "Why am I like Jesus?" And the children replied, "Because you love everybody."

A child once said, "My teacher is great because she turns bodies into somebodies."

TEACHER

Some skilled cooks cook without recipes,
But never in the beginning.
Some skilled builders build without plans,
But never without tools.
Some skilled teachers change their content,
But never without planning.
Some children become skilled climbers, painters,
Storytellers, or puzzle makers,
But never without trying.
No one is born a skilled cook or builder.
We need our plans, tools, and experiences
To help us become skilled persons.
Therefore...

Read your recipe (called "curriculum"),
Plan with your co-workers (called the "community of the faith"),
Teach with good tools (called "resources").
Then you, too will know the joy of being called
An effective TEACHER!

The teacher opened her curriculum book and closed her eyes. "Another Sunday!" she thought to herself, much as a writer faces another blank sheet of paper, a secretary another letter to type, a housewife another meal, the garage mechanic another automobile. Where was her enthusiasm, her interest, her passion? She began teaching because she knew the critical importance of sharing God's story and God's presence and love with children. What had happened to that assurance? Was she tired, hungry, perhaps becoming ill? "God, help me," she prayed, her brief word flying out as an arrow from a bow. She opened her eyes and read the session's plans from her teacher's book and read: "Living is nothing more than doing one thing instead of another." (E.J. Schumacher, <u>Small Is Beautiful</u>) The importance of teaching is that it helps us choose what is important, what is meaningful for one's students and for oneself.

Thomas Merton wrote, "In the end, it is the reality of personal relationships that saves everything." Teachers model who they are, for teaching is incarnational, and an authentic relationship is established when teaching is incarnational.

Learning Opportunities:

1. Brainstorm and discuss the qualities and characteristics of a good teacher:

   Love: a teacher is a warm, loving, accepting person. To be affectionate without being sentimental, to touch when it is appropriate, to show concern with words and deeds is to love. Jesus showed his concern for children when he took the children on his lap and said, "Let the children come to me." (Mark 10:14) The teacher who feels loved by God will share that love with children. We cannot, however, share what we do not have. Therefore, teachers must accept themselves before they can accept children. This means a teacher must have maturity.

   Maturity: a mature teacher knows his/her own needs, has a sense of proportion and humor, and is responsible and dependable.

   A Sense of Joy: the wellspring of happiness is as deep as one's faith.

A Sense of Wonder: firsthand experience with nature and music and art and beauty introduces and feeds the sense of wonder. As Gibran said of the astronomer who may speak to you of his understanding of space but cannot give you understanding, no one can give another a sense of wonder, but it can be shared together.

Knowledge and Know-How: to keep learning and growing, reading and observing, reflecting and experiencing, keep teaching alive.

Good Relationships: good relationships are built on attitudes that are based on the way one thinks and what one believes. All persons need the right climate in which to grow. When uniqueness is appreciated, feelings accepted, and independence respected, self-worth and confidence are the results. Limiting and depriving children of attention or enjoyment is a matter of attitude: "I wish I could read longer, but Karen needs my help right now." Good relationships are based on generosity.

Commitment to God: faith determines, guides, and corrects our thoughts, feelings, and acts. Values, meaning, and trust make living worthwhile. Children need something to live for, belong to, believe in, and make commitments to. An appropriate image of "teacher" is that of St. Christopher carrying a small child on his shoulders safely across the threatening waters. Finally the child can walk alone on the other side of the stream that divided the popular, competitive, materialistic values of the world from Christ and his values.

What is a good teacher? What is the art of teaching? Do we teach to prove our point or dazzle with our brilliance or enable persons to feel and think, reflect and change and grow?

2. Read the following story and discuss examples from the story of a "good teacher":

There was once a teacher of twenty children and she planned and prepared for each child the activities, songs, and stories they loved, and the children were happy to come to church ... all but Sam. Sam came into the room and knocked over the blocks, pushed the puzzle pieces onto the floor, stomped on the baby dolls, and picked the petals from the flowers. When the boys and girls were gone, the teacher said to the other teachers, "I must leave the other nineteen children in your care and help Sam discover that he too belongs." She accepted Sam's feelings, his good feelings and his bad feelings, and said, "I love you because God loves you, but God loves Susan too and I cannot let you hurt Susan." And little by little Sam began to build with the blocks, put the puzzle pieces in the puzzle, rock the baby dolls, and smell the flowers. One day the teacher held Sam in her lap, rejoicing and calling the boys and girls together to celebrate with juice and crackers, for it was as if one lonely, lost boy discovered that he too belonged. And when the teacher told the story of the good shepherd who left his 99 sheep to search for the one lost lamb, they cried, "Tell it again, Teacher!" They did not know that is was their story, but they knew that they had a "good teacher."

3. Complete the following:

   I am here today because...

   Teaching is...

   I would like to dialogue with...(name an author or teacher or any person living or dead).

   The five most important people in my life are ... (behind each name write what they have taught you).

   The five most important books to me are ... (behind each title write what they have taught you or why you choose this book).

   The last book I read or workshop (class) I took was ... I learned...

   I would like to know...

   I learn best by...

   My goals are...

   God's grace has brought me...

   I would like to...

4. Discuss in pairs what you most enjoy about teaching.

5. Write your own personal "Who's Who" (how you want to be known and your major accomplishments).

6. Write an epitaph for your tombstone.

Content

Children

Need

Appropriate

Religious

Content

Singing "I will make you fishers of men" one of the children wondered why Jesus used fishing hooks to "catch" people. Another child after singing "Jesus loves the little children/All the children of the world/ Black and yellow, red and white/They are precious in his sight" called the song "The Stripped Children."

Words are important. Children hearing metaphors such as "The church is God's house" expect to see God there.

One child did and shouted at his mother, as they drove past the church, "There is God!" "Where?" asked his mother, putting on the brakes to look. Carl pointed to the custodian mowing the lawn. Father who lived at Carl's house mowed the lawn. Therefore the man mowing the lawn at God's house must be God.

In stage one of the children's faith development "imagination is the principle medium for ordering the many feelings and intuitions of the world. The meaning-constructive activities appear to be structured primarily in a narrative mode."[1] In stage two children construct the world imaginatively through play, fantasy, and story. Thus, although children do not understand in an adult way, biblical hearing that relates to them will be intuitively and imaginatively experienced on their level.

We are dealing with a paradox: children both understand and do not understand. It is a paradox requiring awareness, appreciation, and prayer on the part of the church educator.

Words are important. Stories "show," describe, concepts rather than defining them. They help children "see" and with their imaginations touch and taste and smell and hear:

> She was a teller of stories. She was a teacher. The children enjoyed hearing her words, seeing her smile and her eyes, feeling her closeness. For a few moments they stepped onto her magic carpet and flew away to Canaan or Babylon or Galilee, places where they had never been before. In those unfamiliar, faraway places they met people, such as Abraham, and Isaac, and Jacob. They saw where Jesus walked and talked, healed and was a friend. They heard the words of Amos and Isaiah. They watched Peter and Paul, and when they returned, they were different from when they had left. One of the children said, "I like Peter. He is like me." One of the children said, "I want to hear more stories about Jesus." One of the children said, "Now I know how Moses felt." One of the children even said, "I heard God speak to me." No one laughed. No one said, "That can't be!" or "How do you know that it was God?" for all of the children had taken the same journey together.

Stories from the Bible answer the basic questions all people ask. "How did the world begin?" (Creation) "Why are people selfish? Why do people disobey God?" (Adam and Eve) "Why do people kill?" (Cain and Abel) "Does God care what we do?" (Noah) "Is God with me?" (Abraham) "How does God speak?" (Moses) "Do other people have feelings of anger and jealousy" (Joseph and his brothers) "Why should I worship?" (Isaiah) "Does God love me? Who is God?" (stories of Jesus).

Church educators of children want them to learn that God loves them through the love of their parents, teachers, and people of their church community. We teach and model this love by preparing the environment and planning the teaching in ways children learn: through doing, through feeling, through the senses.

The particular "words" of the story may not fit within this framework, but the message and experience of the words is universal, timeless, and for all ages and stages. Children can experience a sense of belonging, which is the beginning of a covenant relationship with God. They can experience the grace of God, which is the love they experience at church. They experience judgment and law by expectations and limitations that are put on their inappropriate behavior. They participate in wonder and worship through prayer and song, picture and story, the gifts of nature and of friendship.

They experience creation as part of the environment that they taste and touch and try, and church leaders encourage them to create to "their own size" in ways that are comfortable, joyful, and fulfilling to children.

We know that the stories of the lost coin or the lost sheep are examples of Bible stories the gospel writers told to their first century congregations made up of Gentiles, "enemies" of the Jews, and therefore believed "lost," to tell them that God's salvation through Jesus Christ is for all people, for the story says that the woman and the shepherd did not stop looking for the lost until it was finally found. Children can identify with the woman and the shepherd in losing things. Through their feelings of sadness over the loss and joy in the finding, they enter these biblical stories.

This is the foundation on which we build, for the biblical stories are the core stories around which the community of faith builds its identity and its mission. It is true that there are different levels of hearing a story, and that we peel away layers as the skins of an onion, as we grow. The first level is hearing the story as a story, a story with a plot and characters who act and feel and think. The second level of story is its meaning. What does the story mean to me? To the people to whom it was told? For whom it was written? Interest in meaning comes later, although it varies with individual differences. Around the fourth grade a sense of history comes into children's awareness. The third level is the value of the story. How am I related to this story? How is this story "my" story? What does it tell me about God in relationship to me and my experience? How do I live out the value and meaning of this story in my own life?

Playing games of hiding and being found, finding hidden "lost" objects, pictures to look at and talk about, songs to sing, finger plays to say together and do, books, filmstrips and videos to enjoy, such as "Sean the Bunny"[2] (the story of a lost pet bunny and Charles, the boy who loves and searches for him when he is lost), making cotton sheep, and counting coins are some of the ways to tell and experience the stories of the lost sheep and the lost coin.

It would be unwise not to be aware that we leave out parts of the biblical stories or rather, save them, until they are of meaning and value to the person hearing them. Yet we continue to tell and hear the stories together, for young children too are part of our communities of faith which grow up around the story, the story of God's "beginning" in creation, whose "plot" moves to its "climax" in Jesus Christ, and whose "ending" goes on and on and on.

"I assume that you will keep the grammar, reading, writing in order; 'tis easy and of course you will. But smuggle in a little contraband, wit, fancy, imagination, thought," Emerson wrote to teachers, for it is imagination that sees possibilities in plans, formal, written curriculum and breathes life into teaching in the church. What do you enjoy doing? What do you do well? Find a way to bring that interest, that talent into the classroom, for your enthusiasm and love is contagious. We teach well that which we love.

Children learn that which they love, and love is contagious. What you as a church educator love will spill over, encouraging that same love in others.

When I asked my seven-year-old "fake" granddaughter, Sarah, to go to church school with me, she replied, "It's too dull!" Soren Kieregaard said that to be dull is a sin. To be dull when sharing the good news of God's love is sad and so I told Sarah, "I am sorry. Learning about God, being with God, is the most exciting learning that there is." Teacher, preacher, do not be dull. It is better to be wrong than dull.

It is better to love and celebrate the Bible than to understand it. When children (adults, youth, congregation) are gathered to celebrate the sacred story by which we live and move and have our being, the story, the Bible, comes alive. It becomes our story, our meaning, our mission. The goal of Bible study with children is to help them deal with the "meaning" questions of their lives as they discover meanings in the Bible. To learn "God loves me" is the most important teaching of the Bible.

Celebrating the Bible is not teaching about God but being a participant of that faith story in a relationship of love with God. We "know" another through our relationship with that other. As that relationship deepens, we know the other more fully. Because each of us has our own personal relationship with God, there is a variety, a diversity of understandings of the biblical stories. In the Bible God's people's understanding of God varies, as well. It evolves and changes through their experiences with God. "Bible" means library, different kinds of writing: letters, history, stories, prayer-poems, gospels, etc.

Children find meanings through discovery, exploration, and participation. Using their faith imagination to enter the story, it ignites the inner fire that allows them to feel with a power to persuade, to initiate action, and to heal. It generates feelings, and through their feelings children learn.

Many of us, as adults, see "men as trees walking," until Jesus touches our minds and hearts with the gift of faith imagination to see whole and to see for ourselves. Too many of us have been taught not to create but to copy, to imitate, and when we do, we are blocked from the awareness of our own unique gifts.

There is no impression without expression. Express your love, your trust relationship with God, and prepare the environment in the hearts and minds of your students to experience God's presence and love and to express their response.

The curriculum the church educator uses, any curriculum, is a guideline, a map, but the educator is the one who charts the "course." When we remember that we are created in the image of God, and therefore sub-creators, we can "soar" in our imaginations, for we are kings and queens in the realm where God is Ruler.

Paul Klee, the artist, once said, "Art does not reproduce the visible. Rather, it makes visible." Teaching in the church is an art, the art of making visible the spiritual world, of intertwining the physical-religious world of the Bible with that spiritual world, so that with active imagination we can step into that ancient, oriental, adult world and experience its stories for ourselves.

To keep alive and exercise the imagination is one of the most important tasks of the church educator. Freedom of feeling, thinking, and expression can bring energy, hope, and transformation, as Paul wrote in Romans 12:2a: "..be transformed by the renewal of your mind."

Church school is not dull. Teaching, sharing, expressing our living faith and relationship with God is the most exciting opportunity and work we are given. Teaching is an art in the church!

Learning Opportunities:

1. For evaluating stories and storytelling, ask: What would children hear or feel from this story? What was the purpose for telling? Was the story interesting? What did you most enjoy? Was the delivery helpful? (eye contact, enthusiasm) What did you learn from the telling? Was the story appropriate for the age of audience? How did you feel about the telling? Did the introduction "hook" attention? Was the ending satisfying?

2. In choosing stories for telling, ask yourself: What is the story saying to me? Why is it included in the canon? What does it tell me about relationship with God? Why would I choose to tell this story? What are the images I see?

3. Do an "active imagination" exercise in which you invite participants to become relaxed, "centered," to breathe slowly and deeply three breaths, feet on floor, eyes closed, hands in lap. "Think of someone you love or your entire class and invite them to meet Jesus. Listen to what is said. Observe what happens and respond with your active imagination. See Jesus. See the child. Listen to what Jesus says."

4. Ask participants to choose a partner and talk together about anything related to the visualization. Were there any surprises? frustrations? joys? How did you feel? Extend this when you are in private and have a longer period of time. Be honest, if nothing happened, say so. Each of us learns in different ways and imagination

sometimes needs more time and more practice. Imagination is a gift. "Will" does not always produce it.

5. Have paper and pencils for each person to write 3-5 of the most artistic things about themselves: What is the gift you have been given to share? Talk with a partner you trust about your gift and the restrictions that block you from giving. Take turns. Each person shares for five minutes and at the closing one of them says aloud a prayer incorporating these gifts.

6. Discuss with the entire group by asking: What do the words "Made in God's image" mean to you?

7. Brainstorm the group's favorite Bible stories and why, telling their experiences with that story.

8. Ask participants to write a prayer of thanksgiving for the blessings in their life. Pray a group prayer, each person sharing their individual prayer.

9. Sing "I Love to Tell the Story."

[1] Handbook of Preschool Religious Education, ed. Donald Ratcliff (Birmingham, AL: Religious Education Press, 1988), p. 106.

[2] Sean the Bunny, Elaine M. Ward, (Allen, TX: Tabor, 1981). Filmstrip is out of print.

Death

Children Need Help In Living With Death

"What are you doing, Kathy?" her teacher asked. Kathy looked up. "I'm drawing a picture to send to Muffy." Mrs. Bruce was silent, remembering that Muffy was Kathy's cat that had died last week. Kathy was aware of the silence and replied, "It's O.K. I have her address. How do you spell 'Heaven'?"

What do we say when death invades the child's world? How do we help children live with death? Mrs. Bruce waited, for frequently children supply their own answers, the solution that meets their need.

Many adults avoid speaking about death with children because children do not understand the finality of death and adults do not like to think about that finality.

None of us has a final answer to what happens to people after they die, therefore we cannot help children to "understand" death, but we can help them accept death as a part of living. When a child wants to know what the dead person is doing, the only honest answer is "I do not know," for it is impossible for us to know what life after death will be. Children deserve the truth, yet although we do know, we trust God's love, and can add, "But I believe..." In that trust we can help children cope with their fear of this part of life.

Children learn about death through literature.

Sensitive stories, such as Charlotte's Web, can be introduced to children (third grade). Charlotte, the spider, uses her weaving and writing skills to spin the words "SOME PIG!" and "TERRIFIC" across the pen of her friend, Wilbur the pig, and thus save his life.

Children experience the joy of victory and the sadness of Charlotte's death, for "Wilbur never forgot Charlotte. Although he loved her children and grandchildren dearly, none of the new spiders ever quite took her place in his heart. She was in a class by herself. It is not often that someone comes along who is a true friend and a good writer. Charlotte was both."[1]

Fourth graders and older children (and their parents) appreciate Bridge to Terabithia, the story of two good friends, Leslie and Jess. My son read it to my grandson, Tiuh, when he was nine. At the end of the story Tiuh asked his father, "Why are you crying?"

Emotions over both beautiful stories and death can and should be expressed.

The story is based on the true account of the death of Leslie by lightning and the author's need to make some sense out of the tragic death of her son's young friend, killed by lightning. She wrote the story for herself. Later, when the book had sold millions of copies and readers of all ages had written to her pouring out the pain of their own lives, Paterson wrote, "I keep learning that if I am willing to go deep into my own heart, I am able, miraculously, to touch other people at the core."[2]

She also wrote about writing and reading stories that matter, whose purpose is that children may see the "nature of the game" and "make purposeful moves." "I will not take a young reader through a story and in the end abandon him. That is, I will not write a book that closes in despair. I cannot, will not, withhold from my young readers the harsh realities of human hunger and suffering and loss, but neither will I neglect to plant the stubborn seed of hope that has enabled our race to outlast wars and famines and the destruction of death."[3]

Children learn about death through the sacred story of Jesus Christ.

Such hope brings us to the climax of the sacred story: the life, death, and resurrection of Jesus Christ. When children ask, "Why did Jesus get killed?" we tell of his courage to teach what the people in power did not want to hear. "People in power fear losing their power, becoming so angry and fearful, they kill. Some of those people killed Jesus." "But God is more powerful. Why didn't God stop them?"

Each adult will have his and her own reply. Because I believe in the story to "tell the truth." I tell a story:

In the beginning all was dark and empty and God created sun, moon, stars, land, water, sky, fish and animals. "Something is missing," God thought. "I know! I need people with whom I can have a relationship!" Then God had a problem. Would the people be puppets who did what God wanted or would they have free will, be able to choose? Then God smiled. "I will create them in my image, letting them choose just as I do."

Children learn about death through Christian history.

Christian history reveals many interpretations of the cross. Because I care about children and want them to experience the love of God, and trust that love, and because the doctrine of the atonement is an ancient, oriental, adult concept, I would save Paul's deepened understanding of how Christ died for us until the child is able to understand the richness of metaphor and symbol.

Children learn about death through experiencing the death of pets and the possibility of the death of someone they love.

A child who had the same blood type as his sister who was dying was asked to give his blood. He was frightened because he believed that giving his blood was giving his life for his sister. With tears in his eyes and fear in his heart, he agreed out of love for his sister.
How much more God loves us!

A kindergarten class cared for a bird. One morning the teacher found that the bird was dead. Instead of discarding the dead bird and saying nothing, she showed it to the children who arrived early. All the children who wanted to could hold the dead bird and discover he was cold and stiff and could not breathe or

move. They felt sad and said so. "Why do you think the bird died?"
she asked. They expressed their fear that they had not cared for
the bird properly or that it died of a cold. When the teacher
suggested that he died of old age, his body worn out, one of the
girls said, "That's what happened to my grandma." They put their
bird in a box and buried it in the playground. They talked about the
bird and agreed they would miss it. Throughout the year they
recalled the bird. For many it was there first experience with
death.

We cannot protect children from living with death but we can provide them with the hope of resurrection and trust in our loving Creator.

Learning Opportunities:

1. Discuss possible responses to questions about death, such as: What is death? What happens to people after they die? What makes people die? Did God make him die? It was my fault, wasn't it?

2. Plan a parents' meeting, sharing the stories of Charlotte's Web and Bridge to Terabithwa and their questions concerning how to respond to children's questions about the death of Jesus.

[1]E.B. White, Charlotte's Web (New York: Harper & Row, 1952) p. 184.
[2]Katherine Paterson, The Writer's Handbook, Sylvia K. Burack, ed. (Boston: The Writer, Inc., 1992) p. 32.
[3]Katherine Paterson, Gates of Excellence (New York: E.P. Dutton, 1981) pp. 38-39.

Express

Children Need To Express Themselves

"You shalt love the Lord our God with all your heart and soul and mind and your neighbor as yourself."
(Deut. 6:5)

The roses bloom, the robins sing, the breezes dance with Day,
While World whispers her wonders to the children as they play.

Children express themselves through their feelings, through play, and through creative activities. Through their actions they tell us things about themselves they cannot put into words. It is called the language of behavior. Feelings are the cause of behavior. When children can express their feelings of fear (of being deserted, the dark, being lost, loud noises, high places), of anger and frustration and of joy and happiness, they learn to hope and to cope. Coping is confidence in one's own ability to figure out what to do when you do not know what to do. Coping strength comes from belonging, trust, being loved, and opportunities for expressing themselves.

In a church school class the children were asked to write their own Ten Commandments. One seven-year-old wrote at the head of his list: "Thou Shalt Have Fun!"

The eminent psychologist Rene Spitz studied two groups of children, children in an orphanage without toys and companionship and those in a nursery attached to a female penitentiary with toys and company. The latter thrived, the former barely survived.

Play encourages the spirit of cooperation, of sharing, taking turns, putting oneself in the "skin" or the shoes of another, learning what it feels like to be that other. As such learning occurs, children learn the correlation between feelings and behavior.

What is "creative" is difficult to formulate but certain common characteristics are found in creative people. They are independent, flexible, adaptable, and have an appetite for solving problems.

> *A dab ... a painting,*
> *A block...a tower,*
> *A word ... a story,*
> *A seed...a flower,*
> *Clay ... a statue,*
> *A note ... a song,*
> *In creativity*
> *There is no <u>wrong</u>.*

> *Dorothy gingerly put her finger on the wet, white paint she had spread across the paper as a cloud, a swirling veil, a sudden snowstorm. She giggled with delight and soon the white paint covered her arms and face as well, as she cried, "Look, Teacher, I'm Florence of Arabia!"*

Art expresses feelings, feelings about what is happening, touching the hem of truth.

> *In kindergarten she was told, when she colored, "The flowers are red, the sky is blue, the grass is green and that is the way it is." In third grade she was told, when she drew, "The flowers are red, the sky is blue, the grass is green and that is the way it is." In sixth grade she was told, "Draw whatever you want. Use your imagination,'" and she drew red flowers, blue sky, and green grass ... for that is the way it is.*

That is the way it was. Permanency is past. Growth is change. So give me purple flowers and red sky and yellow grass, for I have seen the world with new eyes, with eyes of faith and imagination, and God's reality.

Look at a Van Gogh or Mattissee painting, a Rembrandt or Renoir and you see the language of the imagination. Children in their youngest years are the most imaginative, for no one has taught them "right" from "wrong" in expression. "Why are you painting the sea red?" asked the adult. "Why are you thinking the sea blue?" asked the child.

Robert Frost asked, "What made me think I could write a poem? You're always believing ahead of your evidence. What was the evidence I could write a poem? I just believed it. The most creative thing in us is to believe a thing in." When children are allowed to "believe in" themselves, to express what they feel as well as see and imagine, the world is enriched by their visions and creations. Creative art is important to positive self-esteem, a sense of self-worth, the most important learning of all.

When creativity is encouraged and fed and practiced, it grows. When it is neglected, ignored, or ridiculed, it disappears. Creativity cannot be taught. It is caught. It is caught where there are exciting, stimulating things to see, touch, hear, smell, and do, where there is trust and respect, laughter and talk, and lots of time, where there is space and interesting materials of paints, paper, play dough, wood, water, books, blocks, dishes, dolls, music, color and beauty and quietness. Creativity needs time for reflection and thought, silence and stillness, for new ideas to slip in and out, to dream and to decide.

Christopher Robin and his friend knew the importance of play.

> *"If I had a ship, I'd sail my ship, I'd sail my ship through Eastern seas." Christopher tells of the waves and the sand and the coconut trees, and grey-blue haze where the sea goes up to the sky... "And I'd say to myself as I looked so lazily down at the sea, there's nobody else in the world, and the world was made for me."*[1]

Children have an insatiable curiosity, a desire and a need to know, to learn. They want to touch, taste, see, hear, smell whatever is present, for real learning is learned through experiences in which the learner is personally involved, in which the learner initiates the learning. The essence of learning is meaning. The mode of learning is play. Through play children are given opportunities to use their initiative, their freedom, and their power of choice.

Growing up without opportunity for play and for dialogue poses the gravest danger for the growing child, for play is a way to symbolization and meaning-making. In play a stick is a symbol for a horse and play metaphors give way to language.

Without playing, creating conversation, listening to others, children fail to develop a sense that they can talk and think things through. So children teach us to play and in play to experience joy. Robert Louis Stevenson wrote about joy: "And the true realism, always and everywhere, is that of the poets: to find out where joy resides, and give it a voice far beyond singing. For to miss the joy is to miss all. In the joy of the actors lies the sense of any action."

It reminds me of the story of the rich dowanger who sponsored scholarships for promising poets.

One year Sylvia Platt was the recipient and was invited to lunch at an elegant restaurant. The poet had never seen such splendor and was both pleased and nervous. At the end of the meal when the finger-bowl arrived, floating on the surface of the water was a lovely yellow rose. The young poet, confused, thought it was an after dinner soup, picked out the flower and ate the petals and then picked up the cup and drank from it. Her hostess, nonplused, with great empathy as well as gracious manners, calmly joined her guest, eating her flower and drinking her "soup."

Through play children explore, experience, and discover the world in which they actively participate. Through play they organize their environment and master their situation. Children need opportunities of time, space, and enriched environment, time to daydream and imagine within their inner world, time and space to explore the stimulating environment of their outer world. They need materials which have order and materials on which they can impose their own order, such as sand, water, paint, clay, leaves, flexible materials to collect, observe, identify, and manipulate.

Through play children learn and polish physical skills; their large muscles by walking, climbing, running, jumping, crawling, and their small muscles by cutting, drawing, manipulating puzzles and clay and other toys, building blocks and everyday materials such as silverware, napkins, buttons, zippers, etc.

Through play children learn the meaning and use of words by using them to communicate. They also play with words. Play provides opportunities for experiencing with concrete objects, persons, and events, which is the basis for learning to read. Reading has little meaning as rote repetition without representative ideas. Jesus described his generation as children shouting to each other, "We played the pipes for you, and you would not dance."

Through play children learn the joy of living, the joy of the dance. We too need to become as little children.

The philosopher George Santayana, lecturing a class at Harvard one spring morning, suddenly stopped in the middle of a sentence, saying, as he looked out of the window, "Gentlemen, I'm afraid that sentence will never be completed. I have an appointment with April." With that the learned teacher left the classroom.

Feeling that what one is doing is fun makes life worth living. The one who never plays reminds me of the Baal Tov Shem walking through the house of prayer and seeing an old man religiously studying his books, reading faster and faster, hour after hour, said, "He is so absorbed in his learning, he had forgotten there is a God over the world." And God looked out at the darkness and said, "I am lonely. I will create me a people with whom I can play."

I have just been immersed in the concept of play. I have read about "play and cognitive development," "play and language development," "play and conflict resolution," "play and self-realization," "play and mastery," "play and emotional development," "socio-dramatic play training," "play therapy." I am sick of play. I know that play educates at a deep level, that the essence of play is treasuring the rewards of doing a thing for the sake of the thing itself, that today's culture is consciously, or unconsciously, hurrying children out of childhood, that children's firsthand experiences are their best way of learning, through their own personal exploration, and then I came across one of my favorite authors. Eda Le Shan had held my hand and engaged my attention with her words while I was a parent and my children were growing up, and her words were as fresh today as they were then, three decades ago.

I still remember one of her classic works, <u>The Conspiracy Against Childhood</u>, and as a director of a Weekday School of children two through six for many years, I used her words often when parents, watching their children play would ask, "But what are they doing?" And over and over again, when they asked, "Don't they do anything but play?" I smiled, because I had a friend, a very knowledgeable authority, Eda Le Shan, who understood children and with her I could respond, "They are encountering life! In a free and open exchange, in a room that offers all kinds of experiences and explorations, they are searching for their own answers to their own vital questions ... questions of such power and significance that such skills as learning letters and numbers become dwarfed by comparison."

Today's children live in a changing world, a world of throw away, disposable, synthetic, fake, a world of television, and violence, and one of the most alarming changes is in the arena of play. Children are losing the spontaneity, the space, the encouragement, and the time needed for play. They attend organized school, organized athletics, dance, art, drama, music lessons, and clubs. Birthday parties have become crowd celebrations. Slumber parties now begin at four! Few children have the time to explore, experiment, discover, daydream, read, or direct their own play. The luxury of free time has become a burden rather than a gift.

What is there for the teenager to anticipate when everything has been tried already? How do children learn to dream, to enjoy the powers of imagination? What will help them cope with everyday problems, when most of their free hours are spent watching television and video? Who will teach children patience in a time of instant food, instant pleasure, instant growth? How will they learn the love and joy that comes through active involvement rather than passive observance?

Children learn from and because of adults. It is up to us to find time and space to model and encourage reading and feeding the imagination through the arts, opportunity to daydream and to relate to persons in trust. We must be trustworthy so that our children can learn the meaning and importance of trust, dependability, forgiveness, and love. We must create an atmosphere that fosters faith, in order that our children have a foundation on which to trust God.

Those who have studied and understand children know that play is children's natural, instinctive way of learning about themselves, their feelings, and their world. Play that is fun, absorbing, and challenging is learning. Through play children learn how to think, to solve problems, to test, try out, and discover. Through play children learn how to enhance their physical growth: to hold, to climb, jump, run, balance, swing, pull, push, and move their feet and arms and legs and fingers. Through play children develop the social skills of living with others harmoniously and creatively. Through play each child in his/her own way finds his/her own answers to his/her emotional problems, for children do not talk out their problems, they play them out, and through play children grow spiritually in wonder, hope, and love.

New ideas begin with play: "What if ... you were a senator...a teacher...a doctor...a parent...a preacher...the bent woman...Peter...Moses?" Each of us, made in the image of God, unique and creative, is a partner with God in creating.

Jesus also said, "Unless you turn and become like children, you will never enter the kingdom of heaven" (Mt. 18:3). Ever since then we have attempted to discern what he meant. He might have meant children at their best are more clear-sighted about spiritual things than adults. Or maybe he was referring to children's dependency and trust, or imagination and delight in "little things," and play. Or perhaps he meant that children have a sense of wonder, are honest and spontaneously laugh or cry, and are alive to the love of God.

Learning Opportunities:

1. Read the following poem and discuss it and the purpose of play:

> *A child set out to discover...*
> *Who am I? Who are you?*
> *What am I suppose to do?*
> *How do I learn? What kind of a person should I be?*
> *Who is God? Why does God love me?*
> *Why are you lonely? Why am I sad?*
> *Why are there people who make me mad?*
> *What can I see and smell and say?*
> *"I will give you the answers,"*
> *Said his friend called Play.*

2. Reflect on the question: What is the challenge for the young today?

3. Recall when you were a child. What was your greatest fear? What is your greatest fear today? When you are afraid, what do you do?

4. List the feelings you see children express. In what way? How do you feel when a child is angry? Recall a time when you were very angry. What did you do?

[1]A. A. Milne, When We Were Very Young (London: Methuen & Co, 1966), pp. 36-37.

Place

Children

Need A

Stimulating

Place

"He shall feed his flock like a shepherd, and gently lead them that are with young." (Isaiah 40:11)

Every child needs a stimulating place to grow. Children are nurtured by their environment. A stimulating environment of interesting people, materials, plenty of time and space will motivate a child more than all the pressures of praise, criticism, or verbal encouragement.

Pictures

A stimulating place includes walls that talk; pictures. Posters and pictures of color and words, as well as children's own paintings and drawings, brighten children's lives, stimulate their imagination, and encourage thinking, feeling, and learning.

The following are several suggestions as to how to use them:

1. Display the pictures near the eye level of children for maximum effectiveness.

55

2. Keep the wall or board simple and uncluttered.

3. Change the pictures each week.

4. Display pictures that relate to the theme of the session.

5. Talk about what the children see: "What is happening in the picture? What do you think might have happened before? What might happen next? If you were in this picture, what would you do?"

6. Use pictures to help prepare children for a new experience or story, such as visiting the sanctuary, having the pastor visit, telling a story about sheep and a shepherd.

7. Introduce pictures to stimulate the imagination, giving the picture a name or title, writing their responses into a story, or playing a game.

8. Study the picture(s), close eyes, tell what is remembered.

9. Place pictures face down on the floor. Take turns acting out the picture without showing it to the class until the correct answer is given.

10. Have pictures on a clothesline and take a picture walk.

11. Take photographs in the classroom to help children recognize and learn the names of their friends. Sit on the floor in a circle with the photos face down. As each picture is turned over, that child is asked to stand up and tell his/her name.

12. Cut pictures into puzzles. Divide into two teams, each team with pieces of a picture to see which team can complete their puzzle first.

13. Draw a mural of Bible stories children have studied.

14. File pictures under categories so that they can be easily located.

Books and Stories

A stimulating place includes books and stories. "He (Jesus) did not speak to them except in parables."

Sharing books and stories with children is sharing a relationship. Reading together is a way of saying, "I love you," a pleasurable way. Books and stories enrich living, providing satisfying experiences and memories. The child's literary needs are fed by trips to the library, telling stories, reading books, dramatizing and drawing plots and people, discussion about specific stories and books in general, and modeling our own love of literature.

Through literature we can encourage instead of correct. I remember saying to my own sons, "Remember what Thumper said: If you can't stay anything nice, don't say anything at all"?

Good literature is beautiful language, a foundation for the love of reading the Bible. We read books to experience beauty and to know we are not alone. A favorite story or book is an excellent companion when we are feeling sad, lonely, even angry. They invite us into "another world," where we might experience compassion, hope, joy, even sorrow by stepping into another's "shoes," as Dorothy in the <u>Wizard of Oz</u> literally did.

Begin with infants. A recent experience of caring for infants under twelve months showed me the pleasure the baby receives from books. Not only the constant chewing of the hardback cover but the illustrations brought smiles to the faces of the very young.

Young child enjoy the rhythm, rhyme and repetition of Mother Goose, poetry, and finger plays. The refrain of a lyrical verse from the Psalms, even before the child understands its meaning, provides pleasure, and old children can memorize and illustrate the words.

Faith, hope, and love are attitudes. Imagination and stories form, feed, and transform attitudes. Books with poetic justice and happy endings satisfy children's need for security and hope.

Some books are classics. The style of their writing and the insights they provide make their reading a delight. They are available in your library or through inter-library loan.

Establish a routine time for reading to all of the children as well as to individual children whenever it "fits" the session.

Art

The children's paintings were displayed on the walls for Open House for the parents to see. The mother looked at all of the rabbits the children had drawn from the teacher's "pattern," all of them alike. She was therefore surprised to hear her child say, "This one is mine!" She studied the picture. It was like all of the others and she asked, "How do you know that it is yours?" The child smiled and pointed to a smudge spot at the bottom of the paper. "I left my mark," he said, proudly.

The Scriptures tell us that God created out of creative energy, "dabhar," the word, and that we were created in God's image. Jesus said, "I have come that you might have life and have it abundantly."

Abundantly ... educators are advocating a return to aesthetics, saying that we are thinking too much and not feeling or appreciating enough, that it is just as important to experience beauty as to know "facts." Children need opportunities to experience aesthetics, to achieve joy that comes from the inside.

Doing things aesthetically is doing them in a way that gives satisfaction. Perceiving things aesthetically is discovering things to enjoy in objects and events. Art is aesthetically enjoyable. It is also physically satisfying and emotionally releasing.

"Look, what I painted for you! It's a beautiful painting!" Carrie called to her mother at the end of the church school hour. It had dots of red and green and yellow blended together and in some places there were blotches of brown. Carrie had painted the picture with joy and love. She had painted the picture for her mother all by herself, so to Carrie it was a beautiful painting. Mother looked at the smile of happiness on Carrie's face. "I did it for you because I love you, Mommy!" Mother listened to Carrie's words and hugged her daughter. "Thank you, Carrie. It is a beautiful painting!"

Susie's mother had the opposite reaction to her daughter's "art." The valentine was lopsided and full of sticky white glue. In one place the scissors had slipped and tore the edge. One of the small valentines was upside down on the heart and one was about to fall off. "Why can't Susie be as neat as her sister? Ann always did careful work," thought Susie's mother, as she put the valentine in the trash.

Art is a wonderful media for children. "I did it myself!" is important for building self-esteem, the foundation block to good learning. Finger painting, chalking, drawing, painting, etc. can also help children express themselves emotionally. "Your painting makes me feel like singing," the teacher observed. "It's a song," Sarah agreed.

Creativity is crushed by criticism or lack of appreciation. Ridicule destroys the incentive to invent or investigate, to initiate or imagine. The important thing about creativity is not what the finished product looks like to adults, but how the child thought and felt, planned and imagined and expressed during the process.

There is a wide gap between the child's self-taught art and the adult's. Size is unimportant in children's art. A tree may or may not be larger than a flower or a house. Objects are not drawn according to their factual sizes or colors but to their relationship to the artist.

Children need the approval of others, especially of those significant person closest to them. Sometimes parents or teachers are tempted to finish or do their children's work, when that work is for display or compared with other competitive work. Children learn from this that winning is more important than worthwhile, worthy work. They take more pride in their own "less adequate" accomplishments than the perfectly finished products done by others for them.

Creative activities, such as art, bring out inner resources, imagination, and self-expression. Mrs. Adams asked one of her children, "Would you like to tell me about your picture?" Kevin looked over from his painting at his teacher and said, "It is not a story to tell. It is a picture to see."

Church teachers enjoy and appreciate children's art rather than interpreting it. A child may be using a color because he/she likes that color or because it is nearest his/her reach. He/she may be drawing cats over and over because the child has discovered a particular way he/she enjoys representing the pet.

What about the child who will not paint? Some children want to paint and do not know how to begin. A sensitive teacher can become aware of these children and know how to encourage each individual child by learning their interests and needs. Other children do not want to paint because they have found other media for expressing themselves. On Sundays many children do not want to paint because of their "Sunday-clothes." The child is always more important than the activity. The growing process is more important than the end product, but children can be protected and taught how to paint without destroying or soiling their Sunday clothing. Older children can be encouraged to paint or to talk about pictures and other art media by telling or reading a story and discussing it imaginatively. "what did you feel? see? think? How would you have felt if you had been ... ? What would you have done? said? thought?"

After discussing thoughts and feelings, concentrate on one theme or idea that seems to emerge that participants could paint or draw and encourage them to do it their own way.

FINGER PLAYS

Children like to move. Their large muscles need to move. With finger plays and active, imaginative movements, children learn while moving. Doing is the way children learn and finger plays provide repetition, making memorizing fun, as well as a way of doing things together. Some finger plays teach concepts.

Finger plays encourage identification through pretending. When children become the father, mother, baby, farmer, builder, minister, animal, they are learning.

BE A CATERPILLAR[1]

Be a caterpillar, (crawl on floor)
Creeping in the sun,
Funny, furry, little fellow,
Loved by everyone.
Sleep inside your spun home, soft and warm and dry, (curl into ball)
To awaken in the spring...a butterfly (fly).

Finger plays also teach sequencing in numbers (1,2,3,4) and concepts of size (small, smaller, smallest), shapes, and place (first, last, before, behind, above, below, under, over).

The children listen and repetition enhances their memory and recall.

FLANNEL BOARD

"My children do not listen to my stories." "I want to involve the students, but I do not know how." "How can I help children relate to this story?" "What are some ways I can teach the concept of stewardship." Using the flannel board is a fun way to help children to memorize, participate, and learn.

Nurturing and strengthening the memory is a worthy task. Flannel board stories help children remember, because they combine seeing pictures, hearing related words and participating in movement. They help the storyteller remember. When the figures are placed in proper sequence, the events happen in natural order.

Flannel board figures encourage children to listen. Not only are children attracted by the colorful figures, something to see, but they are a way to encourage the children to listen. "If you listen to the story as I tell it, you will know where the figures come and I will let you put them on the board as I tell the story again."

Flannel board figures can be used with words to teach concepts. The young children at our church brought their offerings to church school but would lose them among the dolls, dishes, and blocks. We decided, therefore, to place the offering plate on the desk beside the door so that when they entered, they could place their offering in the plate. We were proud of our idea until we learned that the children thought they were paying to come inside the room. At that point the teachers asked me to write a finger play to be used with flannel board figures: a church, Bible, globe of the world, minister, and a red songbook.

IF COINS COULD TALK[2]

The coins we brought to church today,
If they could talk, what would they say?

1. This one might say, "I heat the church or keep it cool."
2. This one might say, "I buy the Bibles for the school."
3. This one might say, "I go around the world to share the good news of God's loving care."
4. This one might say, "I pay the minister to preach, marry, bury, baptize, teach."
5. This one might say, "I buy the books we use to sing and pray."
If coins could talk, perhaps that's what they'd say.

Children become comfortable speaking aloud before others when they have had enjoyable practice. Telling the story with flannel or felt figures provides such experiences.

Shy children can overcome their self-consciousness by concentrating on the story and the flannel figures for telling.

Flannel stories also help children acquire sequential thinking, and also develop the fun of being one in a fellowship of participants.

Below are some clues for using the flannel board:

1. Keep the story simple. Too many characters and movements can be confusing.

2. Commercial figures can be purchased or figures can be made. Older children enjoy making their own figures and flannel or felt board.

3. Felt figures adhere to a felt board better than a flannel board. Choose a heavy-duty flannel, if you are using flannel rather than felt to cover your board.

4. Tilt the board slightly when telling the story to lessen the risk of the figures sliding off of the board.

5. Velour, paper, craft cloth, sandpaper, pellon, flocking can be used as well as flannel or felt.

6. With imagination and practice any story, song, or poem can be told and enjoyed with flannel board figures.

PLAY DOUGH

A stimulating place includes play dough. Play dough releases conversation and exercise for the muscles. Pushing, pulling, and pounding play dough is accompanied by conversation. It relieves tension and anxiety, as children squash and punch and pull.

Children's "finished" products can represent or be abstract, but "I made it!" increases self-confidence.

Play dough can be shared.

"I need some!" Stewart shouts, having just arrived at the table. Sarah breaks off a piece to give to Stewart and there is still enough for her.

It may also offer opportunities for taking turns. A certain number of chairs are at the table to provide for satisfaction in the activity, limiting the number of children playing with the dough at one time.

Play dough can create biblical story props or as in the Nativity story, Mary, Joseph, Jesus, sheep, and shepherds are named and the story can be told or enacted informally.

PUZZLES

A stimulating place includes puzzles that provide a quiet change-of-pace from energetic activities. They provide a sense of self-worth and achievement:

The puzzle pieces fell to the floor, the blocks scattered across the room, the dishes clattered as they were dumped into the dishpan. Alex had arrived! Alex went to the book center where the teacher was reading a book. He listened awhile but it took too long to finish and Alex did not like waiting. Alex went to the puzzle table and sat down to work a puzzle. He smiled as he completed puzzle after puzzle. When he had finished the third puzzle, Alex got up and went to watch some of the children beating the butter. Feeling good about putting the puzzles together, Alex was glad to simply wait his turn.

Encourage children to do things for themselves, such as putting together puzzles, but remember that children learn more from success than from failure:

Susan's teacher moved the piece near to where it fit, but by this time Susan was frustrated and giving up on the puzzle. "How can I help?" asked Susan's teacher. Susan thought a minute. "I know! We can take turns putting in the pieces of puzzle." She smiled at her teacher. "It's your turn!" Susan had solved her own problem!

Learning Opportunities:

1. Invite parents to a meeting in which children and art is discussed in relation to children and the Christian faith, for as we encourage children in their art, which is the expression of each person's own uniqueness, we are

modeling our faith that each person is creative and made in the image of God and that God loves all persons in Jesus Christ. Display all of the work or take slides to be shown to parents or to the class.

2. Take a slow walk. Express: "Stop and consider the wondrous works of God" (Job 37:14). Take time to enjoy the beauty of wild flowers, brooks and streams, fruit in season, songs of birds, fresh rain, caterpillars and cocoons.

[1]Elaine Ward, Be and Say a Fingerplay (Prescott, AZ: Educational Ministries, Inc.).
[2] Ibid.

LOVE

CHILDREN

NEED

LOVE

"We love because God first loved us."

Why do you comfort me?
Why do you care?
Why do you listen?
Why do you share?"

"Child, let me tell you,
Help you to see,
I love you, because
God first loves me."

Teaching is a ministry of love. Love is what makes people know who they are. Defining love is an intellectual enterprise. Love prefers to imagine and experiencing love is a king of magic that lasts for a lifetime that enriches and makes the living of life meaningful.

The mother hugged her four-year-old son. "Charles," she said, "I hope we will always be friends, even when you grow up."' And the child replied, "Even when my feet grow long, Mommie, we'll still be friends."

Children learn love through warm, loving, accepting persons.

The child came crying to his teacher. She put the child on her lap and asked, "Did you have an accident?" She comforted the child and the child trusted his teacher. He felt safe and loved in

her lap. Then the child stopped crying and replied, "Christopher hit me, but I'd like to think that it was an accident, because he's my best friend."
And Jesus said, "As the Father has loved me, so have I loved you."

The door burst open, letting in a gust of cold wind plus a tousle-headed little boy with an armful of brightly colored leaves on tangled branches. "Mommy, Mommy, look what I found back of the brook!" Stevie shouted exuberantly. "Aren't they something? Won't they look scrumptious on top of the piano?" "Steve—oh, Steve, look at your feet! And your grimy hands! How will I ever get things clean?" Stevie stopped in his muddy tracks and a solemn curtain covered his small face, stilling the joyful shouts. The bright yellow-and-red leaved branches dropped in a pile on the floor as he soberly studied his soiled fingers. "I'll go wash 'em, Mommy," he said, starting down the hallway. Then he stopped and looked back at her, the tiniest hint of a smile on his face as he said, "But my heart wasn't grimy. I had a shining feeling all inside me when I found them for you." Mrs. Richmond picked up the branches and, as she did, the sudden misting of her eyes made the colors blur and blend as in an old oil painting. "Stevie—oh, Stevie—come here." She opened her arms wide, branches in both hands. "They are beautiful. So beautiful. Thank you for bringing the bright outdoors inside our house." Boy-like, a moment later, he struggled from her tight hold, squinting as he studied the mud on his hands. "It was kinda messy getting them, though. I'll go scrub!" She smiled, watched him go down the hall, and prayed silently: "Don't ever let him wash the inside shine away, dear God. Just let him keep it always. And please, God, don't let me ever get so involved with worrying over grimy little hands that I forget the shine inside that fills those hands with gifts of love."[1]

Children know how to give and receive love.
When Sarah was three, she sat on the edge of the sink, her feet inside the bowl, turning on the hot and cold water while I watched, not saying a word. At last she looked up at me and said, "I really like you, don't I?" What I heard Sarah say was, "You really like me, don't you?"

What children experience when they are young lasts.
I listened to them argue around the dinning room table whether less money should be spent on the Pentagon, whether the poor deserved "our" money, which political party was "better" and why. Their voices grew louder and the arguments more heated. They were brother and sister and had not seen each other for four years. Would their differences separate them? I smiled, for I knew it would not, because they loved each other.

Love built on trust can survive differences. Henry David Thoreau wrote, "It is strange to talk of miracles, revelations, inspiration, and the like, as things past, while love remains."

Robert Inchausti wrote, "A few years ago I saw Mother Teresa on television. It was just after the Beirut booming by Israel in which so many civilians were killed. She was helping place two wounded little girls into an ambulance when she was accosted by several reporters. One of them asked her if she thought her relief efforts were successful given the fact that there were 100 other children in another bombed-out hospital whom she wasn't aiding. She replied, 'Don't you think it is a good thing to help these little ones?' The reporter did not flinch but simply asked his question again: 'The other hospital has many wounded children, too. Can you call your efforts successful if you leave them unattended?" Mother Teresa ignored his repeated question and, with an obstinacy worthy of an American politician, answered her own: 'I think it is a good thing to help these children.' And then her shoulder sank beneath the weight of the stretcher."[2]

Children can be generous and gentle, sensitive and humble, as well as boisterous, bragging, selfish and self-centered. So can adults. We only disguise it better.

A man sat in the hospital waiting room, tears rolling down his cheeks, his shoulders rising and failing as he sobbed, then moaning as a foghorn wailing in the night. The people in the waiting room were uncomfortable, not knowing how to respond, when a small child squirmed loose from her mother's arms. The toddler played with the ashtrays, the water fountain, the magazines and finally stopped in front of the sobbing suffering adult. She watched seriously and deeply as the tears continued to roll down his face, and then she reached her hand out to touch his face, wipe the tears from his cheeks, and say gently, "All right, all right, all right." The man opened his eyes and saw the child. The shape of his mouth changed slowly. He gently caught her hand between his wrinkled fingers and kissed it.

He was five and he loved the world and all that was in it. He had been born blessed with the gift of loving. He believed that he had the most wonderful grandparents in the world. He loved his father and his mother with a child's trusting love. He was sorry for the stray, hungry animals and the shy, lonely children, and shared his love and his time with them. That Christmas he made a gift for his church school teacher and after she had received it, he received a letter in the mail addressed to him. It was a thank you note from his teacher, signed, "Love, your teacher." His mother read him the note and the child replied, "I do! I really do!" He really did. I know. He was my son.

It was "dear Sarah" who said it, "Someday, when I grow up, I want to be just like you, Elaine." God sends us messages of God's love, and the messengers we call "angels." Sarah was loved and because she was loved, Sarah loved. We were enjoying the circus when suddenly I had a fit of shivers. I had a sudden attack of flu. By the time we reached Sarah's house, I could only fall on the couch, disintegrating as the three-year-old covered me with her constant companion, her blanket, and then Little-Bit, her cat, as her gesture of concern. Sarah, the imaginative one, the lover.

Francesco (five years old) asked his mother, "Whom do you love more, me or God?" The mother replied that she loved him more. To which he replied, "I think this is your big mistake."

Learning Opportunities:

1. Read the following story and think of any students you have encountered who are like Bradley:

He was a "problem" child. He had been a problem in every class since he had entered church school in the nursery. He cried and threw blocks and bit and kicked. He wiggled and giggled and shot paper wads through the church school hour. In confirmation class Jesus' stories of compassion went over his head. The sessions on Christian love and concern for one another were punctuated with the confusion he caused. The teachers shook their heads, planned harder, and loved longer, for he was "one of the least of these my brethren." When the boy was a junior in high school one of his former church school teachers told me about a girl with whom her son had double dated over the weekend. "The girl is handicapped," she said. "She does not have many friends and had never had a date before. Her face is scared and she walks with a limp from an automobile accident." "Who was the boy who dated her?" I asked, causally." "Do you remember Bradley Jones, the one who gave us all fits?" Of course I remembered Bradley Jones, but now I saw him with new eyes, as I silently prayed a "thank-you" for all of his long-suffering teachers who had loved the boy and modeled for him what it meant to love.

2. Pray together: Lord, forgive us for refusing the children, for being blind to their needs, the young and the old, children who are sexually molested, battered to death, starved with hunger, even children neglected by well meaning, wealthy parents, bending them to their own needs, cowed into the acceptance of concepts that are confusing and incomprehensible, causing fear and lack of self-esteem, self-worth, children taught through toys and television that war is acceptable, respectable, and even glorious, children taught taboos and prejudices

contrary to their natural instincts. Help us love them as you love them, in Christ's name.

[1]Author unknown, *The Christian Home,* November, 1964, Nashville, Tenn.
[2]Robert Inchausti, *The Christian Century,* October 16, 1985.